W9-BFG-081

DISCARDED

Counting Coup

Becoming a Crow Chief on the Reservation and Beyond

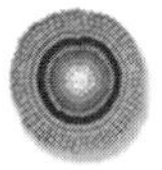

By Joseph Medicine Crow
with Herman J. Viola

NATIONAL GEOGRAPHIC
Washington, D.C.

I DEDICATE THIS BOOK TO MY WIFE, GLORIA;

TO MY CHILDREN

RONNY, DIANNE, GARNET, AND VERNELLE;

TO MY GRANDCHILDREN

KERRY JOE, DEON DREW, RAMONA, DAVID, CHESTER,

TIARRA, KRIS ROBIN, AND R.J.;

AND TO MY GREAT GRANDCHILDREN,

RUTHIE, AARON, ISRAEL, CRYSTAL, AND EVAN

PHOTO CREDITS:
Jacket images: The war bonnet used as backround on the front cover
with bead detail on the flaps and spine is
Joseph Medicine Crow's own, used with his permission;
photograph © 2006 National Geographic Society.
The photograph of the Crow men on horseback is courtesy of the
Library of Congress. All rights reserved

Insert images: author in traditional dress: copyright © Glen Sawnson;
family portrait: National Anthropological Archives, Smithsonian Institution;
young Joe: courtesy Joseph Medicine Crow Collection; Chief Medicine Crow:
National Anthropological Archives, Smithsonian Institution; Yellowtail: courtesy
Joseph Medicine Crow Collection; Agnes Yellowtail: Buffalo Bill Historical Center,
Cody, WY; Dr. William Petzoldt Collection, Gift of Genevieve
Petzoldt Fitzgerald, Rev. W.A. Petzoldt, D.D., Photographer; PN.95.195

Published by the National Geographic Society

Trade edition ISBN: 0-7922-5391-4
Library edition ISBN: 0-7922-5392-2

Cover design by Bea Jackson and Dan Sherman
Text design by David Seager

Library of Congress Cataloging in Publication data available upon request.

Printed in the United States of America

Contents

Foreword

BY HERMAN J. VIOLA

Joseph Medicine Crow and I met for the first time in 1973, when he came to the Smithsonian Institution to do research on his Crow people in the National Anthropological Archives. As director of the archives, I assisted him in his research, and we struck up a friendship that deepened over the years. Indeed, I came to appreciate this remarkable person more and more during my many visits to his beloved Crow country. Thanks to him, each time I would come away with a better appreciation for the Crow people and their place in American history. He showed me some of the special places in Crow country—mountain ledges where Crow boys over the centuries sought their vision quests, the gap in the Pryor Mountains where passing Crow people would leave offerings to their special protectors, the Little People, and of course the Little Bighorn

Battlefield where his grandfather, White Man Runs Him, served as a scout for George Armstrong Custer and the Seventh Cavalry.

During one of my visits to Crow country, Joseph did me the highest honor by adopting me as his brother. He named me One Star, after one of his beloved grandfathers, who played such an important role in his early life. Whenever we communicate with each other, we use our Indian names. He is High Bird, and I am One Star.

My brother and I would like to thank several people who assisted us in telling his story. First is our close friend George Horse Capture, Curator Emeritus of the National Museum of the American Indian, who helped me persuade Joseph Medicine Crow to record his story because it would document such an important time in the history of the Crow people, their difficult transition to life as reservation Indians. We also wish to thank Mr. Tim Bernardis, the Librarian of the Little Bighorn Community College on the Crow Reservation, who helped record some of the stories. Thanks are also due to Sherman and Myrtle Hubley of Billings, Montana. Myrtle Hubley's father, Chester Arthur Bentley, was one of the early Baptist missionaries on the reservation. Myrtle provided records about the establishment of the Baptist mission at Lodge Grass; she located photographs of the mission at the Buffalo Bill Historical Center in Cody, Wyoming; and she assisted us in various other ways as needed to facilitate the project. Finally, we wish to thank Nancy Feresten and her staff at the National Geographic Society for their assistance in publishing this important story.

Herman J. Viola
Curator Emeritus
Smithsonian Institution

Joseph Medicine Crow
Crow Tribal Historian
Lodge Grass, Montana

INTRODUCTION

A Warrior Tradition

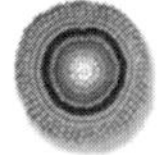

IN THE OLD TRIBAL DAYS, a Crow warrior had to perform four different types of war deeds, four "coups," in order to become a chief. The most important, the most respected coup was to sneak into an enemy camp at night and capture a prized horse, perhaps a buffalo horse, a warhorse, even a parade horse. The daring warrior had to slip into the camp unnoticed and find such a valued horse in front of the owner's tepee.

Usually the horse would be inside a corral or enclosure made of brush, poles, or logs. Sometimes the owner would have tied one end of a rope around his horse's neck and the other around his own wrist. If the horse moved around during the night, the owner would wake up and crawl to the tepee entrance to make sure his horse was safe.

If a Crow Indian, or any other Plains Indian for that matter, was cunning enough to go into the corral, untie that rope, take that horse out of the camp without waking anybody, and bring it back home, why that was an amazing achievement. That coup is called "capturing a horse."

Another coup was to touch the first enemy to fall in a battle. When warriors from two tribes fought each other, the first person knocked off his horse became a trophy, and warriors from the other side would attempt to reach that fallen warrior and touch him with a hand, a riding whip, or maybe the tip of a bow. Sometimes warriors carried a special wand for touching the enemy. This wand—called a coup stick—was wrapped in fur and adorned with eagle feathers.

For a third coup, a warrior could take away his enemy's weapon—his knife, tomahawk, spear, pistol, or bow.

The fourth type of coup, usually the last requirement, was to lead a successful war party. After a warrior had completed the first three coups, sometimes several of each, and had proven himself a good, promising warrior, he would be given the opportunity to lead others into danger. If the war party was successful, if it returned with horses and other trophies and if all the warriors returned home safely, the leader of the war party received credit for a coup.

These were the four coups that a Crow warrior had to accomplish in order to become a chief. There were no shortcuts. Each coup involved risking one's life. Many a young warrior was killed right in front of an enemy tepee while trying to capture a prized horse.

Attempting to count coup on a fallen enemy was also extremely dangerous. Maybe the enemy was just dazed. Maybe he realized he was a trophy, a potential target, and was just sitting there with his gun loaded or his bow and arrows ready to shoot the person who tried to touch him. Even if he was dead, his comrades might be nearby ready to leap on a warrior trying to count coup on their fallen brother.

Attempting to take a weapon away from an enemy also was fraught with danger. He might be bigger and stronger than you, and he might get you instead.

Commanding a war party was an awesome responsibility. When things got really tough, the leader had to make sure that his men could escape even if it meant having to stay behind and give up his own life. All four requirements for chieftainship were difficult to accomplish. Attempting any of them could mean putting your own life on the line.

CHAPTER ONE

Winter Man

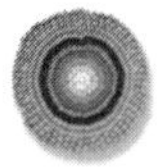

When I was born, on October 27, 1913, there were no doctors or nurses around with their instruments, just a medicine woman who specialized in child delivery. With incense of burning cedar and the singing of sacred songs, I came into the world. I was singing, too, but they probably thought I was wailing.

On the fourth day after a child is born, it is the custom of the Crow people to call in a clan uncle or other important person to give a name to that newborn child, girl or boy. When I was born, there happened to be a Sioux Indian visiting my grandfather Yellowtail, so they asked him to give me a name. He was honored because the Sioux have the same tradition.

"I am glad you asked me to do that," he said. "But I am going to tell you a story first. I have been a warrior for a long time. I came over here to fight you Crows many times, till the war days were over. Seven times you people shot me with bullets and arrows, and each time was wintertime, but I survived all of them. I must have a good life, or a charmed life, or I must be tough, so I am going to give this little boy a name that commemorates my experiences fighting you Crows. I am going to name this little boy Winter Man so that he, too, may be strong, healthy, and withstand many adversities in life." So that was my given name, Winter Man. I carried that name for many years. For short, they called me Winter.

I was raised by many different relatives, but I spent most of my early years with my mother's parents, the Yellowtails, in their log house located about four miles south of the nearest town, Lodge Grass, Montana.

Although my grandfather Yellowtail had not been a warrior, he raised me to be one, to be tough and strong like the old-time warriors. When I was about six or seven, he started my physical-education regimen. I remember it was cold, maybe November, and snow was on the ground.

One morning grandfather said, "All right, get up! Put on your pants and shirt. That's all. Don't put on your shoes. Now, run around the house once, in the snow—barefoot." So I did. I'll tell you my feet were really cold when I came back in.

Well the next day, he said, "Run around the house twice." Then it was 3 times, 4 times, until I got up to 20 times. I had to run around that house each morning no matter how cold it was outside. He gradually saw to it that my feet were tough and able to withstand the cold.

Then one morning he said, "All right, now the next one. Don't put your clothes on. Run over to that sagebrush over there," pointing to a bush about 50 yards away. "Run over there and when you get there, flop down on your back and roll over. Roll over about 4 times one way and then the other way and then come back." I did that. He made me do that every day. The second day, I rolled a little farther—5 times, 6 times. Some days when it was below zero outside, it was hard to do, but the training never stopped. Finally, I had to roll about 20 times through that deep snow and run back to the house. It is a wonder I never got frostbite.

One part of Grandfather Yellowtail's own program for healthy living was to take a cold bath every morning of the year, summer and winter. Naturally, he would take me along. In the wintertime, he had to chop holes in the ice that covered the Little Horn River so he could water his horses. Every morning after opening the holes he would get in and take a dip, and he'd make me get in there, too.

The river water ran really fast past that hole, creating a powerful suction. He would hold me and dip me in and out, and then we'd head for home. The river was about 150 yards from the door of the house. Our feet would have frozen by the time we got back, so we would wear overshoes. But I tell you, some mornings when we got back from our dip, grandfather's braids were frozen stiff like two sticks. Then he would gently thaw out his braids. Otherwise they would have snapped off.

I had to go through that kind of training every winter while I lived with the Yellowtails. I've always been able to withstand cold weather, and I've never been sick. I think the old Sioux warrior who gave me the name Winter Man gave me a good name. Of course, the training of my grandfather Yellowtail also helped.

CHAPTER TWO

Counting Coup

MY TRIBAL ENROLLMENT NAME is Joseph Medicine Crow. My enrollment number is 3378. The first white people who met my people called us Crows, but our tribal name is Absarokee, which means "Children of the Large Beaked Bird." I am a member of the Whistling Water Clan, one of ten clans in the Crow nation. I have lived for more than 90 years on the Crow Indian Reservation.

Our traditional homeland is a vast area that stretches across much of present-day Wyoming and Montana. The reservation is much smaller than that, but it is still a large and wonderful tract of land in the southeastern corner of Montana. Its lush meadows and wooded hills are full of wildlife. Once ideal buffalo country, today our pastures nourish the horses that remain so much a part of Crow life, as well as vast herds of beef cattle that now graze where buffaloes once roamed.

We Crows believe our country is the best place on Earth, a gift to us from the First Maker, who created the world and then divided it among the various peoples who came to inhabit it. Our country is neither too hot in summer nor too cold in winter. It has beautiful mountains and many lakes and rivers filled with clear, cold water.

The First Maker wished to test our courage, so he surrounded us with several of the most numerous, fearsome, and militant Indian tribes on the Northern Plains. As a result, generation after generation of our outnumbered Crow warriors had to defend their homeland against Sioux, Cheyenne, and Blackfeet war parties intent on capturing our splendid horses and our beautiful women. Warfare was our highest art, but Plains Indian warfare was not about killing. It was about intelligence, leadership, and honor.

Before the government established the Crow Reservation in 1884, the Crows had lived as nomads, traveling here and there, hunting buffalo, going on the warpath, capturing enemy horses, counting coup, enjoying their particular way of life. It was a good life, I think. But when the reservations were established, they were required to forget about their old ways and live like white people. They had to start farming, learn English, and become Christians.

It wasn't easy. In their minds, in their hearts, they were still living in the past, still cherishing their traditional religion, philosophy, and way of life. So when the United States Government forbade them to dance, sing, speak their language, or carry on their cultural traditions, the old people would just hide and continue to do things the way they used to do them. For that reason, all the boys of my age on the Crow Reservation were brought up in two ways at the same time. We were raised to be warriors but we were also expected to succeed in the white man's world. In a way, then, I have walked in two worlds my entire life.

I was introduced to my expected role as a Crow warrior very early. In fact, it is my earliest memory and dates back to about 1919, when I was five or six years old. The Yellowtails and some neighbors who lived across the river from us, the Covers Up family, decided to go to the Pine Ridge Indian Reservation to visit the Sioux. We got on a train and went to Edgemont, South Dakota, where some Sioux were waiting for us. They took us in wagons to Pine Ridge.

After a trip of about two or three days, we got to a camp where the Sioux had a big celebration going on. An arbor, a shelter of poles and brush, had been set up to protect the audience from the sun while they watched the dancing. When we got there, they invited us to sit under the arbor.

While we were sitting there watching, a man stepped out into the middle of the dance circle with a little boy all dressed up in a beaded outfit—leggings, vest, and moccasins. It became very quiet. Everyone was watching them. All of a sudden, the man started pointing in our direction.

My grandfather said, *"Hoh!"* meaning "Come," and dragged me out into the middle of the dance arena. I was really scared.

After my grandfather and the Sioux man talked a few moments in sign language, the Sioux man grabbed me by one arm. Another Sioux man got my other arm, and they put me on the ground flat on my back. By then I was kicking and screaming. Then, while they were holding me down, another man picked up the little Sioux boy and sat him on my chest, and the boy began whacking me on the head with a stick. He was counting coup on me.

Coup (pronounced "coo") is a French word that means "to touch." To a Plains Indian warrior "to count coup" meant, literally, "to touch the enemy." To count coup, a warrior might kill an enemy, injure him, struggle with him, or merely touch him. It was only by counting coup that Plains Indian men could become famous warriors or renowned chiefs. Of course, I knew none of this at the time the little Sioux boy counted coup on me.

After hitting me a few times, the Sioux boy got up, and I was allowed to get up. Then the Sioux man took off the boy's beaded clothing and put it on me. Looking back at that day, I guess I was the last Crow on whom the Sioux counted coup. It was a very symbolic moment, a great honor to me and my family. It showed that the Sioux, like the Crow, were keeping the tradition of counting coup alive symbolically even though the old intertribal warfare was over. But at the time I was just a bewildered little boy who was very grateful to return to my seat under the arbor.

Visiting other tribes, even former enemies, was not unusual in the early reservation days. Crows visited the Sioux. Cheyennes visited the Crows. After all, we had a shared heritage and great respect for one another. In fact, members of these tribes would become fast friends and even adopt or marry one another. This happened in my own family when I was 13 years old.

In 1926, there was a Fourth of July Indian celebration at Lodge Grass. Among the visitors was a large camp of Cheyennes, who attended the celebration as guests of the Crows. Among the Cheyenne visitors was a chief named Brave Bear, his wife, Walking Woman, and their young grandson, Charlie. While they were watching the Crows perform the Sacred Pipe Dance, Charlie ran to his grandparents to tell them that he had seen his father standing in the crowd.

The grandparents looked at each other and tried to explain to Charlie that his father was dead and could not be there. But the little boy insisted that he had seen his father and begged his grandparents to come and see for themselves. Just to calm the excited boy, they agreed. Charlie led them directly to a Crow man. Walking Woman looked at the man, gasped, then embraced him and started to cry. Brave Bear was also quite shaken, but he quickly explained in sign language to the surprised man that he looked like their only son who had died recently in Oklahoma. Charlie kept looking at his father's likeness. He was so happy!

The Crow man was John Whiteman Runs Him, my stepfather. He invited the Brave Bears to his lodge for a feast. After the meal a Cheyenne interpreter was summoned. Through him, Brave Bear and Walking Woman informed my stepfather that they wanted to adopt him as their son to replace the son they had only recently lost. This was in accordance with Plains Indian tradition.

When the celebration was over, my parents took the Brave Bears to their farm located at the foot of the Big Horn Mountains, and they stayed with us all summer. Every summer after that they would come back to live with us. When Charlie died, my brother, Arlis, and I became their only grandsons. They loved us, and we would call them grandfather and grandmother in the Cheyenne language. This made them happy!

Many Crow men liked Brave Bear and would come and visit him. They enjoyed his sign language account of his intertribal war days. I, too, enjoyed these storytelling sessions. Fortunately a half-blood Cheyenne woman married to a clan relative of ours was generally around to interpret for us. Through them I heard many good Cheyenne stories. Grandfather Brave Bear was a kind, friendly, and wonderful man. Even after he died, Walking Woman continued to visit us. She died in 1936.

CHAPTER THREE

Old Ways and New

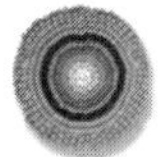

MY MOTHER'S NAME was Amy Yellowtail, and my father's name was Leo Medicine Crow. My father died in 1915. My mother lived to be nearly a hundred years old and died in 1992.

I will first tell you about my father's family. Leo Medicine Crow was one of the four sons of Chief Medicine Crow and his wife, Medicine Sheep. Chief Medicine Crow was born in 1848 and died in about 1920. He was a great man. He had 22 war deeds to his credit, and he was a medicine man and could see into the future.

In about 1863, during one of his vision quests, the fasting experiences that Crow warriors performed to gain spiritual power, Medicine Crow had a vision in which he saw a long object coming up the river running on round legs and puffing smoke like a steamboat. The Southern Bighorn Railroad was built along the river in 1893, and Medicine Crow had seen it coming 30 years before.

Medicine Crow also saw his future house during a vision quest. It was there on top of a hill overlooking the junction of the Little Bighorn River and Lodge Grass Creek, sometimes called Greasy Grass Creek. In his vision he saw a house located by a nice spring. Some 30 or 40 years later, when the Crows were moved by the government to this part of the reservation, he found the spring and built his house right there.

As a little boy, I sometimes stayed with my Medicine Crow grandparents, and I used to play in that spring. I would build a dam with mud and sticks like a beaver, and then I would swim in the pond that I had made. The spring is still flowing, just as beautifully as it did so many years ago. Sometimes I go there just to sit and watch the water and have a nice cold drink on a hot day.

The first Indian housing on the Crow Reservation was log cabins. Later the government started building frame houses for Crow families, and that's what they built for Chief Medicine Crow. These were crude, two-room wooden houses with windows, doors, and floors. Usually there were two stoves in the house, one in each room.

In those days Crow families didn't have furniture. There were no beds. Everyone slept on the floor on blankets. In the morning after we'd come out of the combination bedroom–living room, my grandmother would roll up the bedding and set it along the walls. During the day, we used it as cushions to sit on or rest on. When friends came to visit, they would sit on the rolled-up beds. In those days a bed was both a place to sleep and a couch.

We also ate on the floor. The mother or grandmother laid out a piece of cloth, and we sat around it to eat. No one had tables and chairs. We didn't miss them because we didn't know anything about them. During the summertime the men built a shade arbor of brush outside, and we ate all our meals on the ground under the arbor.

I never stayed very long with the Medicine Crows. I spent most of my time with my mother's parents—the Yellowtails. My grandfather

Yellowtail was born about 1850 and died in 1928. He was not a chief, and he told me that he had gone on the warpath only once or twice. My grandmother, Yellowtail's wife, was named Elizabeth Frazier. Some people called her Lizzie. Although she was half Scot, a quarter French, and only a quarter Indian—she had red hair and blue eyes—she could not speak English. She was an Indian in every way except appearance.

Yellowtail's mother also lived with us sometimes. Her name was Bear That Stays by the Side of the River. She was a real old-time Indian. She kept living in her tepee even after the government built a log cabin for Grandfather Yellowtail. She wouldn't live in a house, even in wintertime. Eventually, when she got really old, somebody, maybe her sons, built her a log cabin. It had a wood stove for heating and cooking, but no floor, no ceiling, no windows. That's how she lived. That house was near the town of Lodge Grass, so later, when I went to school in town, I would stay with my great-grandmother Bear That Stays by the Side of the River.

I also have another set of grandparents—the One Stars. One Star was at one time married to my great-grandmother. When my mother was born to the Yellowtails, she was adopted by her grandmother Emma Chienne and her husband, One Star, who lived just across the railroad tracks from the Yellowtails. Sometimes my mother was known as Amy One Star but her official Bureau of Indian Affairs name was Amy Yellowtail.

When Emma Chienne died shortly after I was born, One Star married a woman named Sings in the Woods, *Ba-le-len Balax-xe.* She was a good-natured, kindly, and always laughing kind of woman. I spent a lot of time during my growing up years with One Star and Sings in the Woods. They had no children except their adopted daughter, my mother, and I was their only grandchild.

One Star wasn't afraid of anything at all. He was a policeman for the Bureau of Indian Affairs and was stationed for a long time in the town of Lodge Grass. I recall the big shining star on his vest and a big pistol on his side. He was a dead shot with that pistol. In those days, Crow Indian men still carried pistols, especially pearl-handled pistols. They would have pistol shooting contests, and my grandfather One Star was good at shooting targets.

I loved staying with the One Stars. Grandfather One Star worked the evening shift policing Lodge Grass. He would go to town and stay there until about midnight, sitting in the pool hall and playing cards while on duty. When it was time to go home, he would cash in his chips.

With his winnings, he'd buy treats for me—candy, apples, whatever. I'd wait up for him, even if it was the middle of the night, because he would come home with a pocket full of candy and one great big Delicious apple. Delicious apples were a new variety then, and this pool hall sold them. Delicious apples became my favorite food.

In his will, One Star left everything he owned to my mother, even though they were not related by blood. He gave her all his land, plus land allotments that he had inherited from his parents and relatives. And he gave me 160 acres, his homestead near Lodge Grass with a house on it. So that's where I live now, the One Star allotment.

As a child I would stay with the Yellowtails for a while, then I'd go over to the Medicine Crows for a while, then I'd come over to the One Stars. I was kind of a mischievous little boy, always getting into trouble. I'd wear out my welcome one place and then I'd go to the other places. But they all loved me, and I learned a lot from each set of grandparents.

I also have some other relatives I call my grandfathers. Take, for instance, Whiteman Runs Him. He was my grandmother Pretty Sheep's half-brother. In Crow Indian kinship terminology, he was my grandfather, and of course I would go visit him. Then I also had another grandfather, Little Nest. He was a half-brother of Grandfather Medicine Crow. During the summer months, when school was out, I would go visit Little Nest in Wyola, Montana.

Although I was raised by pre-reservation Indians, I was also raised Christian. It happened this way. In 1904, the Crow people of Lodge Grass wanted a school like a white man's school, a school where Crow kids could go during the day and then go home when class was over in the afternoon. Until that time, Crow Indian children had had to go to government boarding schools, sometimes far away from home. These early boarding schools were terrible places.

The kids often got sick and died. They were punished for speaking their language. They were terribly homesick.

The elders, including my grandfathers, got together and asked the Baptist Indian Mission Board in Sheridan, Wyoming, to build them a day school at Lodge Grass. After several meetings, the Baptists agreed to establish the school, but they wanted to build a church, too. That is how we got a Baptist mission church and school in Lodge Grass. The church is still there, and that's where I still go to Sunday services.

Anyhow, when that happened, the elders and a lot of other Crows, my grandparents included, joined the Baptist Church in appreciation for the school. Right after that, the Catholics also built a church and a mission, and some Crows joined the Catholic Church. Those are the two main Christian religions on the reservation now.

Although many Crows became Christians, they also kept their traditional religion and just mixed the two together. At the same time that my grandparents were going to the Baptist Church, they were active in the Tobacco Society, which is a traditional Crow religion. It gets its name from the herb they smoke during the ceremony, which is a type of tobacco. During the week, they participated in Tobacco Society ceremonials, and on Sunday they went to the Baptist Church. It's the same with me. I go to native ceremonials. I watch Sun Dances. But I am still a Baptist.

CHAPTER FOUR

Stealing a Beef

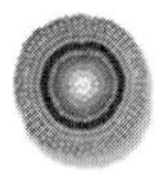

When I was a little boy, I didn't realize I was living on a reservation. I was just having a good time. But looking back, I know it was a tough time for our Crow people. Our tribal population had dwindled down to fewer than 2,000, maybe as low as 1,800 according to the Bureau of Indian Affairs census. The reason for the low population was disease. Diphtheria, tuberculosis, chicken pox, all kinds of childhood diseases had killed a huge number of people. We were down to our lowest ebb.

Even getting enough to eat was difficult in those days. The Crow people are meat eaters, and our primary source of meat had been the buffalo, but now the buffalo were gone. Since we don't eat horses and had no money to buy meat, we had to depend on wild game. But with so many hungry people hunting, there was hardly any wild game left on our reservation—no deer, no antelope, no elk, just rabbits and other small animals. In order to eat meat, then, we had to butcher a cow on the sly, one that belonged to a white rancher.

That was stealing, but we felt justified because the big cattlemen who grazed their beef on our reservation were paying us hardly anything, maybe two or three cents an acre to feed thousands of head of cattle. So we felt that since they weren't paying a fair price for our grass, we had the right to eat some of their beef.

It wasn't easy to steal a beef. You had to be careful. My grandfather One Star was great at that. He'd take off by himself in the middle of the night, especially when there was no moon. Somehow he would come back with beef. I think he must have used a rope. He didn't dare shoot a gun because the cowboys watching the cattle would hear the sound and come running.

The ranchers knew the Indians were stealing beef because occasionally they'd find a cowhide lying around. They didn't mind losing a few cows to the Indians because the price for cows was low at the time, maybe $25 a head. Besides, the Indians usually did the butchering at night, and it was hard to catch us at it.

One time, however, one of our neighbors did get caught. He was a one-armed Crow Indian who lived in a shack across the river from us. His arm had been shot off in a fight with cavalry near Fort Custer many years before.

One day this old man went up to the Wolf Mountains in daytime and killed a cow. A line rider for the Spear Brothers Cattle Company must have heard the shot. When he came over, he saw the old man skinning the cow with his one hand. He watched him cut open the inside of the cow and grab the liver. When it's still hot, the liver is very sweet, like sugar. The old people would eat it raw. So this old man cut off a piece and began eating it. The cowboy watched him eating that bloody, raw piece of liver, then shook his head in disgust and left. He must have been thinking that the poor old fellow was so hungry he was reduced to eating raw meat, not knowing that what my neighbor was eating was the tastiest part of the cow.

Usually, a man would go alone to steal a beef, but sometimes two really close friends or relatives would do it together. Once you had a beef, you had to hide, somehow, otherwise word would get around, other hungry people would ask for some, and it would be all gone in no time. My grandmother used to dry slabs of the meat. She would air the meat at night, and then early in the morning she'd put it away so magpies or ants couldn't get it. In time the meat would be dried and could be saved to eat later.

Sometimes we didn't have any meat at all. We then had to live on berries, cherries, and other foods that the old folks gathered during the summer. I remember eating just bread and potatoes when times were tough.

The Yellowtails were pretty good at growing a garden. Grandfather Yellowtail raised nice big potatoes. My grandmother would help with the gardening, and she also raised chickens and turkeys. Most Crows, especially the older people, didn't go in for raising chickens. It was too much work. They would do without eggs. But my grandmother was good at raising turkeys and chickens. So sometimes we had turkeys and chickens to eat, but often it was just biscuits and gravy.

Although the Yellowtails were pretty self-sufficient, they needed to buy some things at stores in Lodge Grass. Trying to communicate with the white clerks who could not speak Crow was often very difficult. One morning my grandmother Lizzie and I were in the Stevenson Trading Post in Lodge Grass when Flat Dog, an old Crow man, came in. He asked my grandmother how to say "eggs" in the white man's language. "I don't know," she told Flat Dog.

At that point the clerk in the store asked Flat Dog what he wanted. Flat Dog looked around but could not see any eggs to point to. When the clerk again asked Flat Dog what he wanted, the old man took the clerk by the hand and led him to the middle of the store. Taking his blanket from around his shoulders, Flat Dog laid it on the floor, and shaped it into a round, nestlike form. Then, he squatted over the blanket nest and cackled like a chicken. He then got up, pointed into the imaginary nest, and said, "Papoose."

The clerk laughed, walked behind the counter, and brought Flat Dog some eggs. Flat Dog put his money on the counter and turned to leave. As he walked past my grandmother and me, he said in Crow, "This white man is really dumb. I had to talk to him like a child."

CHAPTER FIVE

A Life Outdoors

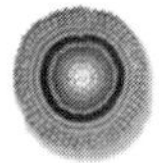

ALTHOUGH THINGS WERE TOUGH for the old people, for us kids, life was good. We played lots of games and had no worries. In the wintertime our favorite game was spinning tops on ice. We made the tops out of rocks—pointed rocks with rounded tops. We'd get a top started and then use whips to keep it spinning around. We broke into teams of two, maybe four, boys. Each team would try to get its top to knock over the other team's top, like a couple of football players banging into each other. The top that fell over would lose.

In the spring when the ground was muddy, we had mud fights. We would get a willow or choke-cherry branch, one that had a good swing to it. We'd put a fistful of mud on the end of the stick and fling it. We'd divide into teams, and those who got hit by a mud ball were out of the game. The game ended when all the boys on one team had been hit.

We liked to have mud fights at night. Both sides would build fires. All the boys would make mud balls and put them in the ashes. Red-hot embers would stick to the mud balls, and when we threw them, they would fly like comets or missiles. Whenever one hit somebody sparks would spray. Our name for this game was *shibia ahshua,* which means "hunting with mud" or "fighting with mud."

Another popular game, for both boys and girls, was shinny. It was something like field hockey, with two teams using sticks to get a ball into the opposing team's goal.

Sometimes we made baskets out of wire and tied them onto the end of a stick to play a game like the Iroquois game lacrosse. We used the basket on the stick to sling a ball about the size of a softball made out of buckskin and stuffed with fur from a deer's tail. These were great balls. They bounced and would really go when you hit them.

We'd fish too, especially in the spring when the water was high and catfish and bullheads would go up the Little Horn.

In summertime we would throw arrows. We didn't use bows. Our arrows were like spears with feathers on them to make them fly straight. Crow kids still do that today.

One of our favorite summertime activities was swimming. Before we could go in the water, however, my old great-grandmother Bear That Stays by the Side of the River would say, "Be sure to give the water monsters some food." Then she'd give me a little sack of food, and before we swam I would throw a chunk or two of meat into the water. This pleased the water monsters, and it was all right then to go swimming.

We'd race each other across the river or up and down the stream. Then we would play the old stick game. We'd have ten to twenty sticks and choose sides. Somebody would throw the sticks out into the river, usually at the bend where the water slowed up and was deep. Then we'd swim out there. You'd grab all the sticks you could find then swim back and count them up. The team with the most sticks won.

Yes, life was good for Indian kids in those days. But then fall would come, and school.

CHAPTER SIX

The Baptist School

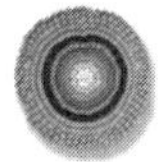

I WILL NEVER FORGET my first day at school. I was six years old, and I rode the four miles that morning with Aunt Agnes Yellowtail, who was about twelve. The Baptist day school was a one-room building with one teacher who taught all the grades for about 25 or 30 Crow students. The teacher put me and two other children at a table built like a sandbox and let us play.

Of course, I didn't know any of the rules. I didn't know we were not supposed to talk, so I started talking away, jabbering in Crow. I called over to my aunt Agnes who was on the other side of the room. The teacher came rushing over and said something to me in English, but I didn't know what she was saying. When she went back to teaching, I started talking again. The teacher came running over again, but this time she grabbed me and shook me quite severely, hard enough to scare me.

I started crying. As I was crying she continued to shake me. The more she shook me, the more I cried. This went on for awhile, the shaking and the crying. Finally, I got loose from her and ran around the desks with her right after me. She finally caught me, and then she shook me some more. We were now standing in front of the class.

As I stood there, I finally quit crying, but I started hiccuping. And every time I hiccuped, she'd look at me and say, "When you hiccup, say excuse me!" At first I did not understand what she wanted. I finally I got the message, but when I tried to say "excuse me" in English, I couldn't say it. She would insist I say excuse me. When I didn't, she would shake me some more, and I would cry some more. This went on forever it seemed.

For the rest of the day I just sat real quiet at the table feeling pretty bad. I hated that woman right from the start. When I was little, my great-grandmother Bear That Stays by the Side of the River had said to me, "If you're not a good boy,

I'll give you to the white people." That old lady instilled in me the idea that white people were to be feared, that they were dangerous and mean. And my experience with this schoolteacher proved to me that my grandmother was right. For a long time after that, I would just keep quiet, not do anything the entire day at school. The teacher ignored me for the rest of the year.

For three years I stayed in that Baptist mission school. The mean old teacher left and a new one came. Most of the teaching consisted of putting me at a blackboard drawing and copying the A, B, C's, 1, 2, 3's, and so forth. I did not learn much of anything at all.

CHAPTER SEVEN

Racing

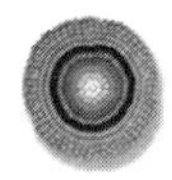

SCHOOL DIDN'T IMPROVE MUCH during this time, but summers got better and better. During the summer we all rode horses. We'd spend a lot of time out in the hills catching colts and yearlings and breaking them. Sometimes, especially at night, we would slip out to the big cattle outfits and rope calves or steers and ride them. We also raced our horses. Crows raise great race horses. We'd race each other all summer on the straightaway benches, the areas of flat land out in the hills.

Kids never gambled on the horse races, but the men did. They'd gamble their saddles, their horses, all their money, anything they had. I remember my uncle Bob Yellowtail came without money to a big horse race on the opposite side of

Lodge Grass. He pulled out his watch, a real fancy watch, put it in the pot, and lost it.

I learned a lot about riding horses from my grandfather One Star, who raised all kinds of racehorses. He made a jockey out of me when I was only about eight.

There was an important horse race at Crow Agency, and somebody had put up a live cow as the prize. The racetrack was a short one, about 500 or 600 yards long. About 30 good horses—most specially trained to race short distances—were entered in the race. My uncle Carson Yellowtail owned one of the fastest horses. Named Colonel T, it was a thoroughbred. A man at St. Xavier owned a half-brother of Colonel T. Another half-brother was owned by someone at Black Lodge. The Crooked Arm boys also had a half-brother of Colonel T they called Messenger Boy. These were all real fast, short-distance racehorses. They always won the big races at Sheridan, Gillette, Miles City, and Billings.

Anyhow, my grandfather One Star had this tall, long-distance racehorse he named Glass Eye because it had one gray eye and one black eye. I think it was an English jumping horse. It was the biggest thoroughbred I had ever seen. One Star decided to run old Glass Eye in that big race. Glass Eye could easily run two miles, and he was hard to beat at that distance, but he had no chance in a short race like this one.

As I stood there watching, Grandfather suddenly said, "Get on him!" I was afraid, but I climbed on Glass Eye. "All right, let's go." Grandfather led me to the edge of the long line of horses so I would not be right in the thick of it. I was riding bareback. My short little legs were way up high on Glass Eye's ribs.

"Grab some mane," Grandfather said. "Wrap your hands around the mane and hang on. Hold on to the reins with your right hand. Hold him tight." After I did that, Grandfather said, "Don't worry about whipping Glass Eye, he'll run by himself."

We stood there awhile, and suddenly, "bang," someone fired a pistol. Off we went. Old Glass Eye took off, and I think my feet were flying straight out for a while, but I just closed my eyes and hung on as tightly as I could. I was afraid to fall off. I couldn't pull him back, couldn't do a thing. I opened one of my eyes a little bit and then closed it again.

When I finally opened my eyes all the way, I saw Glass Eye was heading right for a gully—a big, wide gully. Hard as I tried, I couldn't turn him one way or the other. I was sure I was going to die, but that old horse jumped and sailed clear across that deep gully. People didn't believe a horse could jump that far. Anyhow, I came in last. Old Glass Eye was just warming up when the race ended. That was my first experience riding a racehorse. When we got back to camp, somebody told my mother that I had been in the big race, and she almost cried.

From then on I was Grandfather One Star's jockey. He had a small sorrel that was hard to beat at two miles. I rode that sorrel for several years and won every race I entered. Sometimes we would go clear to Buffalo, Wyoming, something like 300 miles from the reservation, for a horse race.

I remember One Star buying me my first saddle. He came home one midnight carrying a large gunnysack. He opened it, and out fell a brand new saddle. I sat on that saddle all night.

CHAPTER EIGHT

Ghosts

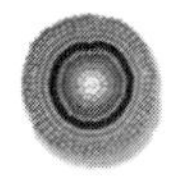

MY GRANDPARENTS INSTILLED many fears in me. Once I confronted three of those fears—ghosts, white men, and Sioux—at one time. They killed me (or I thought they did), but I came back to life. Here is what happened.

When I was about ten years old, I started having trouble breathing through my nose. My grandparents thought that some object had gotten into my nostrils, so they took me to the Federal Indian Hospital at Crow Agency. That's when it all started.

As we entered the hospital, a tall, stout nurse appeared. She was a Sioux, an enemy. She looked into my nostrils and then took me to see another person I feared, a white man doctor. This white man put some sharp knives on a table and put something over my mouth and nose. It smelled terrible. Soon I started feeling numb all over. All I could move were my fingers. The sounds in the room started fading away. Yes, I thought to myself, now these two feared enemies were killing me. Then I was gone.

When I woke up, I was in a bed in a strange room all alone. It was nighttime, and the hospital staff had turned off the lights. As I lay there, the thought came to me that the third danger would now come, a ghost would appear. Crow people at the time believed a hospital was a place where people came to die. They also believed the ghosts of the dead remained in the hospital for a few days after they died. Now was the time for ghosts to come around. I pulled the covers over my head. Although I was terrified, I finally fell asleep.

When I woke up the next morning, there across the room was a ghost lying on a bed. He certainly looked like a ghost to me, with his bluish white skin, his hooked nose, his long, tangled white hair, and his white beard. His gaping mouth was wide open. This ghost had no teeth!

I jumped out of my bed and ran out into the long hall, screaming, "Ghost! Ghost!" As I dashed for the door at the end of the hallway, I could hear heavy footsteps behind me. They came closer and closer. Then the steps caught up with me, and I was lifted off the floor. It was my enemy, the big Sioux nurse. She grabbed me and dragged me back to my room. She pushed me in and held the door shut so I could not get out.

When I finally calmed down, I edged back to my bed and cautiously peeked at the ghost, who was sitting up in bed and vigorously eating his breakfast. After he finished eating, he looked at me with his watery blue eyes and said in the Crow language, "Little boy, do not be afraid of me. I am just an old white man and . . ." I took off again. If there was anything I feared worse than a ghost, it was a white man, especially one with long hair and a beard.

After I was returned to the room a second time, the white man tried again to reassure me that I was in no danger. "What is your name?" he asked in the Crow language.

"Winter Man," I replied, "but I am also called Joseph Medicine Crow."

Then the white man asked, still in Crow, "Are you Chief Medicine Crow's grandson?"

I said, "Yes."

"I know him quite well," the ghost said. "I went with him on the warpath against the Sioux several times."

Despite our harrowing introduction, the old white man and I became good roommates and, later, friends. He was Thomas H. Leforge, a man known among my people as "the white Crow Indian." His Indian name was Horse Rider. As a young man he had left his white family and married a Crow woman. When his wife died, he had gone to Alaska and become a whaler.

Horse Rider told me many stories about the old days, about going on the warpath with my grandfather. I found some of his stories hard to believe, especially when he told me of seeing fish as big and long as our hospital wing. He was, of course, talking about whales he had hunted in Alaskan waters, but he was unable to explain himself clearly to me because there is no word for whale in the Crow language.

Thomas Leforge had come back to the Crow people in his old age. He had come back sick, so he was taken to the hospital and put into my room while I was asleep. As it turned out, I had needed an adenoids operation, but of course I did not know it at the time. Our paths crossed many times before he died. He always wanted to tell stories, but we children did not pay much attention. Why listen to a white man tell stories when there were so many tribal storytellers around?

CHAPTER NINE

Stories

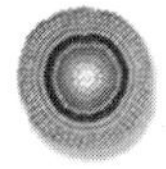

MY GRANDFATHER YELLOWTAIL lived along the Little Horn River, and there were lots of old chiefs living in that valley. So many chiefs lived there that it was known as the Valley of the Chiefs.

Chiefs were highly respected by the Crow people because they had earned their right to leadership on the battlefield. You did not get to be a chief by being popular or because you came from an important family. You could become a chief only by performing the four required war deeds. For each deed, a warrior would be praised and led through the village. His clansmen basked in his glory, and dances were held in his honor. The successful warrior could tie an eagle feather to his hair or attach wolf tails to the heels of his moccasins as symbols of his military exploits, which were recognized and honored by all.

Within three miles of us lived about ten such famous old warriors, including the great chiefs Flathead Woman, Arm Around His Neck, Not Afraid, Old Crow, and White Man Runs Him. My grandfather One Star lived there, too.

During the sweat bath seasons in the fall and early spring, Grandfather Yellowtail would invite these old warriors to our house. I heard legends, myths, and regular stories from plenty of other people, but the war stories, the important stories, I learned from those old chiefs. Often they would correct each other. Sometimes one would say, "That's not the way I heard it." He would then tell his version. That way I sometimes learned several versions of the same story.

Telling stories was important to those old people because everything they valued from the pre-reservation days was gone except their memories. They loved talking about the good old days when there were buffalo to hunt and they could enjoy the traditional life of the Plains Indians. Back then, of course, the chiefs had been the big shots, the leaders.

But all of a sudden, when the reservation was set up, everything had come to a halt. Now a white Indian agent was boss. Chiefs were no longer chiefs. They were nothing. I think that's why they were always talking about the past, reliving it.

After awhile, the Crows began composing songs for their old chiefs. They're called honor songs. When they had a gathering they would sing these songs. The first was for my grandfather Chief Medicine Crow. The idea spread quickly and before long all the great chiefs had honor songs. We still use them to this day.

Those old chiefs enjoyed getting together for a sweat bath. It allowed them to shut out the white man's world and be Indian again. Each day one of them would host a sweat bath. On the days our neighbor across the river, Chief Flathead Woman, would be the host, I would listen for his call, and when I heard him holler, I'd run and tell my grandfather Yellowtail. "He's hollering for us to come!"

"Well, let's go," Grandfather would say. "Saddle up and let's go across the river."

On the days it was our turn, toward evening Grandfather Yellowtail would start building the fire for his sweat bath. Then he would climb up on a hill and holler long howls: *"Heyyyyyyyyyyyy."* He would holler several times, and the neighbors would hear him two, three miles up and down the river. Then, after awhile, here they would come on their horses. Sometimes one or another of them couldn't make it, but those at home would all be there, usually six or seven of the old chiefs. Then, while the fire was heating the rocks, they'd sit down and start telling war stories.

The old chiefs weren't the only storytellers. Grandfather Yellowtail was a great one himself. He would often tell stories in the evening. Sometimes visitors would come and spend the night, and they'd tell stories, too. I heard many stories during cold winter nights. Some were simple legends, but most were true stories.

Another good storyteller was my mother's grandmother Kills in the Morning. She lived to be 117 and died in 1932 or 1933. The strange thing about her was that her hair never turned white. It stayed black her entire life. She was blind for a long time. Because she was blind, she didn't know the difference between night and day. Sometimes she would talk all night. She would wake up and start telling stories, recalling the adventures of her younger days. She would talk for hours.

I still have vivid memories of some of the stories she told me, like the time that the stars fell from the sky. Kills in the Morning was a young girl that night, but the memory never left her. The stars began falling just as it got dark, she remembered. The stars were streaking this way and that way, so many that they lit up the sky. It seemed that some of the stars were landing on the nearby hills. The people in the village were terrified. The camp criers ran through the village and told everyone to put out their campfires, get inside their tepees, cover themselves with their buffalo robes, and pray. They told them not to look up at the sky. Something was going to happen.

Soon the whole camp was dark and quiet. Kills in the Night went into her tent, but she was too curious to stay under her buffalo robe. She stuck her head out from the bottom of the tent and watched the meteor shower. She said the stars continued to fall for several hours and then quit. Nothing bad happened to the village, and life returned to normal, but the Crows never forgot their frightening experience. They named it "The Night When Stars

Started Falling." This was a worldwide event that occurred in 1833. Kills in the Night was probably 13 years old at the time.

The stories I liked best were those told about the experiences and adventures of great Crow heroes, like Wise Man, or *Bachay Balat-Chia* in Crow. Wise Man lived in the mid-1800s. He was highly intelligent and could easily control animals and humans.

One day in early spring some Crow men were discussing which wild creature was the smartest, the wariest, the hardest to catch. Some claimed it was the coyote. Some said it was the mountain goat. Others said it was the magpie. Finally, it was agreed that the sandhill crane was the most difficult creature to get hold of. "No one has ever captured one alive, and no man ever will," the warriors agreed.

At this point, Wise Man interrupted the discussion and said, "I am ready to bet everything I own that I can catch a sandhill crane alive!"

Immediately his challenge was answered by matching bets—a horse for a horse, buffalo robes for buffalo robes, weapons for weapons. When the bets were agreed upon, Wise Man told his

This is a recent picture of me in traditional regalia about to enter the dance arena at the Crow Fair, the spectacular powwow held annually in August on the Crow Reservation. I am holding a dance stick representing the horses I captured from the Germans in World War II.

This 1926 photograph shows my mother, Amy White Man Runs Him, and my stepfather, John White Man Runs Him, in Washington, D.C., where a group of Crows was appearing in a rodeo. My mother is holding my cousin Beauford Yellowtail. Behind them is my brother Arlis. I stayed home that summer, preferring hunting and fishing to traveling. The picture of me (inset) was taken at the Baptist mission school in Lodge Grass.

My two grandfathers, Chief Medicine Crow *(left)*, a warrior of great renown, and Yellowtail *(above)*, who taught me to be a warrior.

Horses were always an important part of my life. This picture, taken by the Reverend Petzoldt, a Baptist missionary, is of my cousin Agnes Yellowtail tending some of the family's horses. Agnes and I often rode together to the mission school in Lodge Grass.

This drawing by Chief Red Horse shows Sioux warriors counting coup on U.S. cavalrymen during the Battle of Little Bighorn. My grandfater White Man Runs Him was one of the six Crow scouts with the 7th Cavalry that fateful day in June 1876.

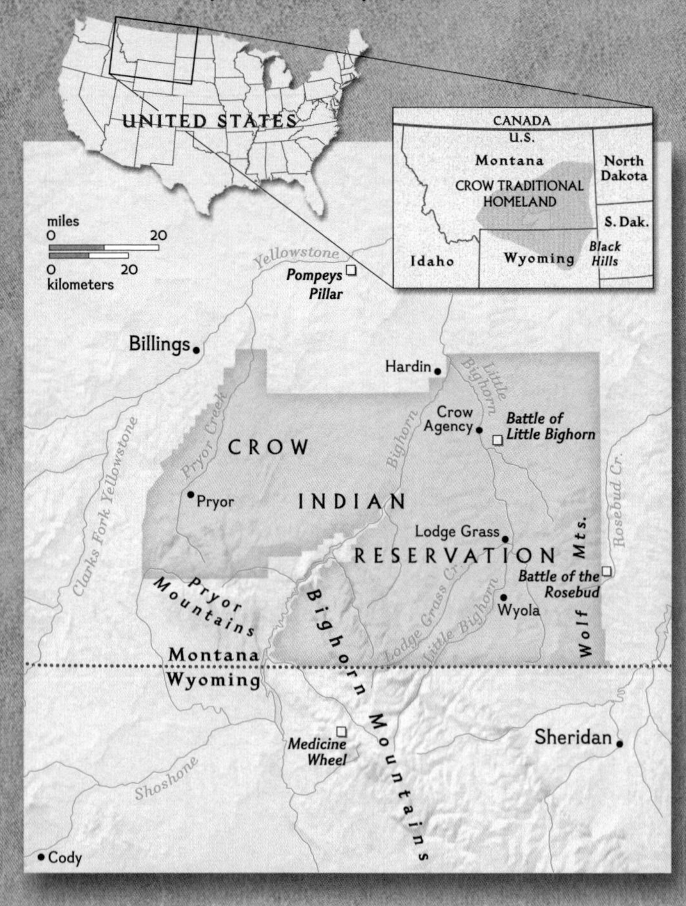

A map of the Crow reservation, where I have lived most of my life.

doubting companions he would return in a few days with a live crane.

Wise Man then left the village and sneaked into a nearby swamp where he knew cranes nested in the spring. He watched the cranes as they went about their daily activities. Then, waiting until the mother cranes left their nests in search of food for their chicks, he took off his clothes and hid in the water near several nests. When he spotted the mother cranes returning, he submerged himself in the water, using a hollow reed to breathe through.

The cranes were indeed wary. They flew around for some time before cautiously landing near their nests. When all was calm, Wise Man emitted a feeble chick call. One crane, apparently thinking that one of her young ones had strayed from the nest, started wading in the water toward Wise Man. As she got close to him, he grabbed her legs and carried her to shore. He tethered the thrashing bird so it couldn't get away and brought her to his village. After collecting his winnings from his astonished friends, Wise Man released the grateful crane, which immediately returned to her chicks.

Another test of Wise Man's ingenuity occurred when a Sioux war party spotted him walking alone in the Black Hills. Wise Man sought refuge on a high point along a rocky cliff. There was no way for him to get down without being seen. The Sioux knew he was trapped, so they took their time climbing toward him, planning to count coup on him.

But Wise Man was making plans for a dramatic escape. He spread his blanket on the ground, then took two slender but strong tree limbs and tied the four corners of the blanket to the ends of the crossed limbs. He grabbed the middle of the crossed tree limbs and, forming a sort of parachute, jumped from the high cliff and floated gently to the valley below.

The Sioux warriors charged into Wise Man's hiding place, but the Crow man was nowhere to be found. They looked over the edge of the cliff and saw, in the distance, Wise Man's dust as he sprinted away from them. The Sioux warriors must have shaken their heads in disbelief, thinking that the Crow man had used some sort of powerful magic in making his escape. They had no idea that Wise Man had invented a crude parachute and simply floated away.

CHAPTER TEN

Public School

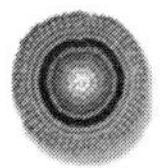

ONE DAY, DURING MY THIRD YEAR at Baptist school, the door flew open and in stormed One Star. He was a big, tall man, kind of rough in his ways. He walked up to my desk, yanked me out of my seat, and said, "*Hoh!* Come! This is no good. I'm going to take you to the white man's school in town. You're just wasting your time here. You're not learning anything. You've been coming here all this time and still can't speak English at all. I need you to interpret English for me, and you can't do it. Come!" Then he walked me out of the room. The teacher just stood there and never said a word.

Well, One Star took me to the public grade school in Lodge Grass. The grade school had two rooms. In one room were grades one through four. The other room had grades five through eight. One Star opened the front door and just pushed me in there. I tried to run out, but he held the door shut, and I couldn't open it.

In the meantime, the teacher came to the door and hollered something, so my grandfather opened the door. He could understand English but couldn't speak it very well. She told him that I needed a doctor's certificate before I could come to that school. "Come on," he said. "I'm going to take you over to the doctor." We went right over to Doctor Taggert's office. He checked me over and said, "Okay." He then gave a note to my grandfather. We went back to the school again, and I went in. By now, it was late afternoon, and I finished the day rather quietly.

This was a tough time for Indians to go to public school on the Crow reservation. The State of Montana had agreed to let Crow Indians attend public schools because the tribe had given two sections of every township to the county. This was a considerable amount of land, 50,000 acres. The white people in Lodge Grass did not like this decision and objected strongly. They felt that Indians shouldn't be going to school with their children. "These Indians," they said, "are dirty and covered with lice. They are so dumb the teachers will have to spend more time with them and neglect our kids."

Of course the parents' anger and prejudice rubbed off on the kids. When I arrived at public school for my first full day, the teacher assigned me to a desk in front of Theresa Lynde, the meanest little girl in town. Theresa had a safety pin, and when class started she began sticking it in my back. Just in and out, in and out, all day, 40, 50 times. I was afraid to say anything. It was just as bad as my first day at the Baptist school.

By the time I got home to Grandmother Bear That Stays by the Side of the River's house that afternoon, my back was hurting all over. My great-grandmother was waiting for me, anxious to know how things had gone. "How was the white man school?" she asked. Usually when I came home from school, my great-grandmother would have biscuits and fried potatoes ready so I could make a sandwich for my after-school snack. When I came in that day, the biscuits and fried potatoes were ready, but I wasn't hungry. I just flopped on the floor and sat there. "What's the matter?" she asked. "Did the white boys fight you or do something to you?"

"The white man's school is no good," I said. "Look at my back." I couldn't see it, but it was hurting. She took my shirt off and shouted, "What happened? You've got little red marks all over your back! Did somebody scratch you? Did something scratch you?"

"No!" I tried to explain about this little girl poking me with a safety pin, but before I could finish telling my story, I broke down and cried. Then my great-grandmother started crying, too. She knew there was nothing she could do to help me. She was more scared of white people than I was.

The next day, of course, I didn't want to go back to that school. But my great-grandmother insisted I go. "If you don't go to school, they'll send you to a boarding school far away someplace." So I went back.

Somebody must have said something to the teacher, however, because she moved me to another desk, and it was all right from then on. But I was in the first grade again. I was now about ten years old and still couldn't read, couldn't write, couldn't even do my A, B, C's or my numbers. The teacher spent a lot of time with me trying to help me catch up.

The following year my younger brother, Arlis, also attended public school. He was a big boy, much larger than I was, and the school got us mixed up. They put him into the second grade and me back into first grade. That was all right with me, but after a while the teacher realized my brother couldn't do second-grade work, and so we switched places. They put him in the first grade and me into second. That was all right, too.

Part of it was our fault. We Crow kids stuck together in school and only used English when we absolutely had to. We watched each other. If we saw one of our Crow classmates trying to speak English to a white kid, we would say, "Look at him, trying to be a white man." We would tease him. Sometimes we would beat him up. We were afraid to use the English language, so we punished ourselves.

Finally, I made it to the fourth grade. Although I was now doing well as a student, I failed fourth grade because I skipped school on the final examination day. I didn't know it was going to be exam day. One of the older Crow boys in the class,

Martin Spotted Horse, suggested we play hooky. "I have some money," he said. "Let's sneak out and go to the butcher shop. I'll buy some weenies and bread, and we'll go into the hills and have a picnic. Let's go."

He was much older than I was. He must have known we were to be tested that day, and he didn't want to take the examination. I liked the idea of a picnic, so we took off. We got on our horses and sneaked away into the Wolf Mountains. We played around, roasted our weenies over a fire, and had a good time. The next day at school the teacher handed out the report cards. Kids were saying, "Oh, I passed! I passed!" When I got my report card, it said, Not Passed. Martin didn't pass, and I didn't pass. We both flunked fourth grade, and I slipped back another year.

As I made my way slowly up the grades, the conflict with white kids continued. Every recess we had fights. After school we did the same thing. If Indian kids were found in town after dark, the white kids would beat them up. We would have pitched battles.

There were five or six Belgian boys living on a farm below Lodge Grass, and we'd pick on them.

As soon as school was out, we'd jump on our horses and head for the stockyards down by the railroad tracks. The Belgian boys had to walk along the tracks to get home, so we'd wait for them. Finally, they got smart. Their mother was a great cook. She'd make them a bunch of extra sandwiches for their lunch. Then, when we stopped them, they'd reach into their lunch boxes and give us each a sandwich. After that we'd put on a big front to them just to get those sandwiches.

We Crow boys were always hungry. We had to take our own lunches to school in those days, but we were so poor we never had enough to eat. My great-grandmother would fix me a couple of biscuit sandwiches with fried potatoes. That would be my lunch. We would carry the sandwiches to school in a little white salt sack tied to the saddle. When we got to school, we would tie our horses under some nearby trees and go in, but we would leave our sandwiches on the saddles—we were ashamed to take those potato sandwiches into school.

However, a lot of magpies lived in those trees, and they learned to fly down and peck holes in the sacks and eat our sandwiches. More often than not, those magpies got my potato sandwiches. Then I would come home hungry. That's why we were happy to get the sandwiches from those Belgian boys.

CHAPTER ELEVEN

The Battle of Little Bighorn

MANY OF THE STORIES I HEARD at the sweat baths were about the Battle of Little Bighorn or, as it is often called, Custer's Last Stand. This terrible battle, fought on June 25, 1876, is one of the most famous in American history. On that day, the 7th U. S. Cavalry led by George Armstrong Custer attacked a large village of Sioux and Cheyenne Indians camped along the Little Bighorn River in southeastern Montana.

With Custer and the 7th Cavalry were six Crow scouts. One of them was White Man Runs Him, who was the brother of my grandmother. This made him, in the Indian way, my grandfather. He was the longest lived of the Crow scouts and died in my parents' home in 1927.

The other Crow scouts were White Swan, Goes Ahead, Curley, Hairy Moccasin, and Half Yellow Face. I knew all these men well except White Swan, who died before I was born, and Hairy Moccasin, who died in 1922. I greatly enjoyed listening to them talk about their scouting for Son of the Morning Star, the Crow name for George Armstrong Custer. The Sioux and Cheyenne called him Yellow Hair.

According to their stories, Custer did not take the advice of his Crow scouts, who told him to wait for reinforcements before attacking the Sioux and Cheyenne camp. Instead, he divided his force of 700 soldiers into three parts and attacked right away, with disastrous consequences. Custer and the 200 soldiers under his immediate command were all killed. The rest of his army survived because reinforcements arrived in the nick of time.

The Indians in the village that Custer attacked were led by Sitting Bull, Crazy Horse, Lame White Man, and other important Sioux and Cheyenne leaders. The week before, their warriors had defeated an even larger force of U.S. soldiers at the Battle of the Rosebud. Therefore, when Custer attacked, the Sioux and Cheyenne were not frightened. They counterattacked, inflicting one of the worst defeats the U.S. Army ever suffered at Indian hands.

White Man Runs Him was six-feet, six-inches tall, handsome, and a likable young man. After the battle, he was interviewed by more writers than all the other scouts put together. He was eventually regarded as the most reliable informant about the battle.

After I learned English at school, I sometimes was the interpreter when white people came to ask White Man Runs Him questions about the battle. He became very impatient with these people because they often asked him leading questions and seemed to want him to confirm what they already knew, or thought they knew, about the battle.

One question frequently asked was whether Custer was drunk the day of the battle, which might help explain his disastrous defeat. Many soldiers, scholars, and others claimed Custer did not drink whiskey and did not allow his officers and soldiers to do so either, but White Man Runs Him insisted that Custer's soldiers had been drinking whiskey that day. I remember one time he told me to tell the white man interviewing him to leave because it was obvious he did not believe what White Man Runs Him was saying. He told me in Crow, "Send him home. He doesn't want to know the truth." After that White Man Runs Him often refused to speak with white people about the battle.

Interviewers often asked why the Crow scouts survived when Custer and his men were all killed. According to the scouts, as they approached the enemy camp, Custer saw that two of them had gotten off their horses and were removing their military clothes and putting on their traditional Crow clothing.

"What are they doing?" Custer asked Mitch Bouyer, his interpreter for the Crow scouts.

When Bouyer repeated the question to the scouts, Goes Ahead pointed his finger at Custer, and said in Crow to Bouyer: "Tell this man he's crazy! He's no good. Tell him that in a very short time we are all going to be killed. I intend to go to 'the other side of the camp'—to the afterlife—dressed as a Crow warrior and not as a white man."

When Custer heard this explanation, he got very upset. He yelled something like: "Tell those superstitious Indians to leave! I don't want that defeatist attitude around my soldiers. Their job was to find the Sioux, and they did that. We'll do the fighting if they are so afraid of the Sioux."

According to White Man Runs Him, Bouyer told the scouts: "You are fortunate! He says you can go now. You have completed your work. Go now! Hurry! Don't stop! As for me, I cannot go. I am in the Army and I must stay." The scouts took Bouyer's advice and left. Bouyer was killed with Custer. The Crow scouts survived.

White Man Runs Him was a person of great spiritual power. My favorite demonstration of this power occurred in June 1927 when a movie company was filming a silent Western in Lodge Grass, not far from the battlefield. The film was called *Red Raiders* and starred Ken Maynard, a top cowboy-movie hero of the time.

About midday a thunderstorm suddenly came toward the set, with lightning flashing and a gale-force wind blowing. The director became very upset because the sudden storm would ruin the set and the cameras. Henry Pretty-on-Top, the Crow man in charge of the Indian cast, saw how upset the director was becoming. He went to him and said that the tall Indian playing the head chief was a medicine man who could make the storm go the other way.

With an offer of a bonus if he could save the set, White Man Runs Him walked toward the coming storm. Then he stopped, raised his right arm high, and sang his power song. As he waved his arm to the north we could see the storm, which was now approaching with increasing velocity, suddenly swerve to our right and roar away.

As a youth, White Man Runs Him had sought vision power by fasting and praying. He received the power to perform difficult feats. No doubt his "medicine" had protected him during the Custer fight, and it was still with him 51 years later.

I have had a lifelong association with the Battle of Little Bighorn and its participants. I can still recall riding horseback all over the grounds as a boy and seeing the bones of the horses killed in the battle. One of my relatives had a ranch adjoining the battlefield. Whenever we visited him, he would take us boys there and show us pieces of military equipment still lying scattered on the ground.

In June 1926, when I was going on 13 years old, there was a magnificent commemoration of the 50th anniversary of the battle. Thousands of people on foot, on bicycle, on horseback, in wagons, and even in a few automobiles converged on a hill just north of the battlefield fence. The main event was a reenactment of the battle.

What a spectacle! Hundreds of horseback riders were raising clouds of dust and filling the air with yells, war whoops, and gunshots. The black powder smoke from the guns added to the thick dust that covered the battlefield. I was excited and thrilled and then completely scared. I would take off as fast as my horse could run and then stop to look back. It all seemed so real!

Later that evening there was a big celebration at the Indian camp. People gathered to see a victory dance. One by one a Sioux or Cheyenne veteran of the battle of 1876 would step forward and loudly proclaim that he was called so-and-so. Wearing his old fighting regalia and brandishing a weapon, he looked fearsomely magnificent.

There was hushed anticipation. Then with a piercing war whoop he would go into a lively and dramatic pantomime, demonstrating his encounter

50 years earlier with a brave soldier whom he had subdued and counted coup upon, earning a war deed. As drummers burst forth with the old warrior's battle song, he would lead a victory dance followed by his female relatives, each emitting the piercing Cheyenne or Sioux women's trill.

Afterward, the aged warrior would slowly walk back to his place in the circle, visibly shaken with emotion. No doubt, to him, this was still quite real. There had been no time to perform war recitals the day after the victory in 1876.

That ceremony had a powerful impact on me, an Indian boy not yet in my teens. I felt tremendous pride that my own grandfathers had once been great warriors and chieftains. The memory of that moment has stayed with me the rest of my life. Later, as a soldier in World War II, I knew that I, too, must fight honorably and bravely, like a Plains Indian warrior.

CHAPTER TWELVE

The Little People

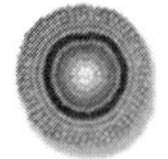

In my youth, wise elders told us that the more you seek to understand the essence of the four basic principles of life—earth, water, fire, and air—and how they interact, the more power you acquire. For our whole history, and even today, young Crow men have gone into the wilderness to fast and pray to the First Maker, the giver and author of life, in order to obtain visionary power. The more power the young man received, the more difficult and seemingly impossible were the feats that person could accomplish. These spiritual people, whom non-Indians often call "medicine men," could do wonders. Yes, they could cure the sick, walk on water, turn daylight into darkness. They could do things that seem miraculous.

To us Crow people, the earth is Mother, the mother of all humans and their animal relations. And all the ancient ones, whoever they were and wherever they lived, knew of special sacred places where the supernaturals could be found. Some of these special places are large. Others are small and appear unimportant. It is in such special places that the Little People live.

The Little People are a combination of spiritual and human beings. They have a capacity to become human yet can quickly disappear. They can also take the shapes of animals and birds. Most often in stories they appear as owls or snakes. The Little People are not imaginary beings. They are real. Even non-Indians have reported seeing them. The early white men who came to Crow country, the trappers and the fur traders, called them Mountain Dwarfs and described them as small and ugly. We have two names for them: *Awa-kulay,* "keepers of the land," and *Awa-kolay,* "those who live in the earth."

I have never seen any of the Little People myself, but those who have, describe them as about three to four feet tall. They are well proportioned and have long, black unbraided hair. Often they wear clothes of buckskin, but sometimes they wear modern clothes. Their faces are rather grotesque, which apparently keeps people from getting close to them. They seldom speak.

One of the special places where Little People are found is the Medicine Wheel, a holy site in the Big Horn Mountains where many Crow boys have gone for spiritual help. The most famous of the Crow men who received special blessings at the Medicine Wheel was Long Hair. As a child he had very scraggly hair, and he felt ashamed of his appearance. When he got older, he went to the Medicine Wheel to fast and to seek help from the Little People. They took pity on him and adopted him. After living under the ground with them for a while, he returned to the Crows as a great medicine man. His power was in his once-scraggly hair, now grown long and luxuriant. It kept growing longer and longer.

"My fathers," he told the Crow people, "told me they will come and get me when my hair measures over one hundred hands in length." As his hair grew longer and longer, he kept it in a braid that he folded and carried in a knapsack on his back. To keep it from getting too long too soon, his wives would sometimes cut his hair while he was sleeping.

One day, when the tribe was camped at the rock the Crows call Where the Mountain Lions Sit—the white people call this rock Pompey's Pillar—Long Hair summoned the leaders of the tribe to his large lodge for a smoke and a conference. As the pipe went around, he sat at the back end of the lodge counseling them.

When the pipe had made several rounds of the room, Long Hair paused. "Now," he said, "the time has come to measure my hair." As he said this, he unpacked his hair and passed it to the man next to him, who began to unfold it, passing it to the next man in the circle. The men kept passing Long Hair's hair until it was completely unfolded and went clear around the circle.

All the while, he kept reminding his chiefs of the goodness of the Great Spirit, of the good place in which they lived. He told them never to sell their land. He gave them other words of wisdom.

"Now," he said, "I am going to take my hair back, but as the end passes each of you, cut a piece off with your knife. Put that hair of mine in little pouches, and keep it there. That is my medicine, my power. Keep a piece of my hair, and you will enjoy a good life. You will be healthy. You will have good fortune. My hair will protect you—you and your relatives and their descendants. I myself have no children, but all the people of the Crow Tribe are my children. So protect the pieces of my hair, keep them holy, take good care of them."

The men did that. Some cut longer pieces than others. When his hair finally came back to him, there were still about nine feet left intact. Long Hair was pleased. "It is good," he said. "Now my people are rich, a big tribe, scattered in different locations. That is the way it should be."

He preached for a while longer and then said, "I'd better rest a bit." He had a backrest made of willow branches. He leaned back and closed his eyes. As he slept, the men continued smoking and talking. Finally, they were ready to go, but they didn't want to walk out on him while he was sleeping. After waiting a little while longer, one of the men next to him said, "We are going to go." But Long Hair didn't move. He was dead. He had died while they were talking. The Great Spirit had taken him to the happy hunting ground or wherever such men deserve to go.

At the end of his speech to them, Long Hair had said, "When my fathers take me, the Heart of the Mountain will also die." At that time the Heart of the Mountain, a peak near Cody, Wyoming, was pointed at the top just like a heart is pointed. All hearts are shaped the same way. Even the heart of a tiny bird like the chickadee is shaped like that, and so are the heart of a buffalo and the heart of a fish.

After burying Long Hair somewhere secret, his people remembered what he had said about the Heart of the Mountain. The chiefs told some of the young men, "You go up there and see what has happened." The mountain was about a day's horseback ride away. When the young men got there, they could see that there had been a big landslide, and a part of the mountain had slid off. The dust was still swirling in the air. They rushed back to the camp and reported. "Yes," they said, "part of the mountain has died. It has tumbled down." What was even more astonishing, the men reported, was that they could see Long Hair's profile in the new shape of the mountain.

His profile is still there. Whenever I visit Cody, driving from the Crow Reservation, I can see the Heart of the Mountain clearly for 20 miles, and there is Long Hair's profile. There is a hump that must be the knapsack that carried his hair. You can see his eyebrows, his nose, his lips, and his chin. You can see pine trees that are his hair. He's there. So that is a sacred piece of land to the Crows. They go there to fast.

I think the Little People created Long Hair's statue. They did it to remind us of themselves and the Crow Indian whom they adopted. It takes a long time to build a big statue, but this was done in a matter of minutes. One time I went there, and I could see water coming down the side of his face. Maybe it was snow melting. It seemed like Long Hair was crying. It made me feel funny, so I took off. Maybe he was feeling sad about something.

◆

We Crows have another special place. It is a gap, a passageway in the Pryor Mountains on our reservation. The place is named Arrow Rock, and it is where the Crows first met the Little People. The meeting took place around 1730, before the Crow people got horses, when they arrived in their present land after their long migration on foot across North America.

The caravan included many dogs carrying packs or pulling travois. A travois was made from a pair of sticks. The sticks were tied at one end to a dog's shoulders. The other ends dragged on the ground, with a seat made of hide or webbing holding them together. Babies and little children often rode on a travois when the villages moved from campsite to campsite.

As the caravan passed through the narrow gap in the Pryor Mountains, a dog pulling a travois with a little boy on it chased a deer and disappeared. The dog later returned but without the boy. His family searched and searched but could not find him. After a few days, the procession continued, but the boy was never forgotten.

Years later, a man walked into one of the Crow camps. He told the people that he was the little boy who had disappeared that day. Relatives came and examined him closely. His sister, now a grown woman, remembered her brother had a scar on his leg. Yes, the scar was still there.

The man, later called Four Arrows or Sacred Arrows, said that small human beings had found him after he fell off the travois and had taken him into their cave lodge. The little humans raised him, taught him secret mysteries of the land, and gave him supernatural powers. After he had grown into a man, it was decided that he should return to his own people. Before leaving he was permitted to choose one of four sacred medicine bundles placed before him. A little bird told him which bundle to select. This particular medicine bundle turned out to be especially powerful.

Sacred Arrows told the Crow people that Pryor Gap was the home of the Little People. He advised the Crows that whenever they passed through the gap on their travels they should place rocks at the base of a high cliff overlooking the valley as a prayer offering for their safe journey. Men must shoot arrows into the crevasses of the jagged cliff face for the *Awa-kulay* men to find and use, and they should leave offerings of buffalo and elk meat for them to eat. Women must place beads, bracelets, and other jewelry at the foot of the cliff for the *Awa-kulay* women to find and wear.

The Little People lived in the Pryor Gap area until the 1890s, when the Chicago, Burlington, and Quincy Railroad decided to build a tunnel right through sacred Arrow Rock. All the noisy activity, especially the dynamite blasting the tunnel through the rock cliff, drove the keepers of the land north into Canada. The Crow people have regarded this tunnel as a curse ever since. The railroad line only used the route until 1911, when it was suddenly abandoned, but the tunnel remains.

Now that Pryor Gap is again quiet, it appears that the Little People have begun to return to be with their Crow relatives. There have been many recent sightings throughout the Crow Reservation. One Little Person even held a woman by her hand and asked her to follow him, but she got scared and ran away. Some children told their parents that when they were playing at a park near Lodge Grass some ugly children tried to play with them, but they chased them up a tree.

My niece, a college professor, saw one of the Little People while returning home one evening after a school meeting. He was sitting on a blanket near the side of the road, and her car headlights shone right on him. He waved to her.

"I was shocked," she told me. "I guess it was like seeing a flying saucer. Anyhow, what really surprised me was his appearance. I had always assumed the Little People were Indians, but this one looked like a little Mexican with a sombrero and pointy shoes."

Little People stories even appear in local newspapers. A Crow woman tired from a hard day working at Crow Agency was in her car driving home to Lodge Grass when a summer thunderstorm erupted, making it difficult to see. Suddenly, she saw a small man wearing very colorful Elvis Presley–style clothes pushing a wheelbarrow along the interstate highway. The vision passed so quickly she thought she had imagined it, but that evening her sister, who drove the same way home, reported seeing the same little man. When they told the story to a white farmer who lived nearby, he reported that sometimes his wheelbarrow would disappear, but it would always reappear as mysteriously as it had left.

If the Little People have indeed returned to Crow Country, it is a good thing. They are the special protectors of the Crow people. Mother Earth is under serious stress these days, and so are her native peoples. The Little People have been kind to the Crows. They have saved us from harm. They watch over us. They have helped us keep and preserve our beautiful land. As Sacred Arrows told the Crow people, as long as we continue to respect the *Awa-kulay,* as we long as we bring stones and other offerings to Arrow Rock, *the Awa-kulay* will protect us. "By doing it that way," the Little People had told him, "you will mark that we are the keepers of the earth. We taught you. We saved it for you. You cannot be pushed off."

CHAPTER THIRTEEN

Boarding School

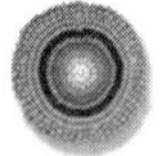

By the time I finished public elementary school in Lodge Grass, racial tension was at its worst out here, so very few Indian children attended Lodge Grass High School. They would go to off-reservation boarding schools, which had improved a lot since their early days. They weren't perfect, but they were better than having to deal with white kids at the public schools. The only Crow students at Lodge Grass High School at that time were two basketball players, my uncle Tom Yellowtail and Pete Left Hand. And this was in a town in the middle of the Crow Indian Reservation!

Well, I was sick of fighting every day so I told my family that I wanted to go away to school. We went to Crow Agency, the headquarters of the

Crow Reservation, and I put in my application with the government education official there. He sent my application to a school in South Dakota, Flandreau Indian School. We waited and waited. Finally, just before schools were to open in the fall, word came that Flandreau didn't have room for me.

I was disappointed and didn't know what to do. It was getting too late to apply somewhere else. Luckily, the Reverend W. A. Petzoldt of the Baptist mission at Lodge Grass heard about my problem, and he offered to help. "I can send you to Bacone," he said. "Bacone is a Baptist-supported Indian school in Oklahoma. And," he said, "I'll send some other Crow children, too."

As it turned out, quite a few of us, about 15 from Lodge Grass and 1 or 2 from other districts on the reservation, went to Bacone that year. This was 1929, and I was about 16 years old. At Bacone I entered eighth grade. Wallace Iron was also in the eighth grade.

Going to Bacone was a real eye-opener for me. The students there were from 30 or 40 different Indian tribes across the country. Until then, my knowledge of other Indians was only of the

Cheyenne, Piegans, and Sioux, who lived near us. It was meeting the kids from other tribes that got me interested in collecting Crow stories because the kids from other tribes would ask me about my tribe. By then, my English was getting pretty good, but I still preferred speaking Crow when I could.

I went back the next year, and I kept going back. I finished high school in 1934 and junior college in 1936. During my years at Bacone I participated in everything. I sang in the bass section of a men's singing group called the Redmen Glee Club. Every spring we would go on tour. We performed in Texas, Kansas, Missouri, and Florida. We performed at the 1932 World's Fair in Chicago. I also took piano lessons, played the saxophone, and was a member of the football pep band and the school orchestra.

I also participated in what athletics were available at Bacone. I played basketball, two years in high school and two years in junior college, and I boxed when I was a freshman. Boxing was a big thing at Bacone, but after a couple of fights I quit.

I got hit between the eyes and had a headache for a week. I took part in track activities. I especially liked throwing the javelin. I was also a pitcher on the high school baseball team.

For three summers—my senior year in high school and my two years in junior college—I worked at eastern boys' camps, one summer in New Hampshire and two summers in New Jersey. I was an instructor in Indian crafts and lore. In New Hampshire I learned how to paddle a canoe. I had never seen a canoe before. I also learned how to shoot a bow and arrow at camp. After the kids went to their cabins for the evening, I would slip over to the archery range and practice.

As far as schoolwork was concerned, I did well except for freshman algebra. But Wallace Iron was a pretty good student. He did quite well in algebra, and he would coach me along. In a little while I caught on and we began to compete with each other, not only in algebra but in other subjects as well. Right from the ninth grade I started earning good grades. But Wallace quit high school after his freshman year, and the others dropped out, too, until I was the only Crow there. Even alone I held my own. Every year at Bacone I made the

Oklahoma high school honor roll. I did well in junior college also. I majored in science and took courses like botany, biology, and geology. When I graduated from Bacone Junior College in 1936, I was pretty high up in my class.

When I returned to the reservation that summer, Dr. Petzoldt said, "How about going on to Linfield College? I'll get you some money." Linfield College is in Oregon. Like Bacone it is affiliated with the Baptist Church. I enrolled there as a junior and graduated two years later, June 30, 1938. I was the first male Crow Indian to graduate from college. The first Crow woman was Joy Yellowtail, who graduated from a college in California in 1937.

When I was leaving to attend Linfield College in August 1936, my Cheyenne grandmother, Walking Woman, was staying with my parents. As I was putting my suitcase into the car just before sunrise, Walking Woman heard the activity and woke up. She came outside and asked where I was going. My mother told her that I was going away to college in Oregon. The old woman stood there and looked at me intently awhile. Then she stepped forward and turned me around to face east. As I stood there looking across the Little Bighorn River to the horizon, she burst into song. It was a wailing type song that I had never heard before, but it is something the Cheyennes and Sioux do. I did not know if she was singing or crying. It was kind of a mixture. At the end of the song, she gave the Cheyenne woman's trill. Then she pushed me and said, "Go!" This was the traditional way Cheyenne women had sent their husbands and sons off on the warpath in the old intertribal war days.

I can still hear her voice to this day. At Linfield things could get pretty tough, and I was ready to quit many times. I had a hard time with accounting. Genetics was rough too. But then I would remember my Cheyenne grandmother sending me off to war. I would remember that, and I would try again. That memory kept me going through all my school days, and it gave me encouragement during the Second World War, when I was an infantryman in Germany. I could almost feel that dear old lady singing and crying like the day it happened.

CHAPTER FOURTEEN

Strong Medicine

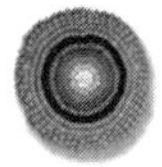

THE WARRIOR TRADITION of the Crow people occupied my thoughts when I was inducted into the army at Fort Douglas, Utah, in 1942. After graduating from Linfield College, I had enrolled in the University of Southern California to study anthropology. But now Uncle Sam needed me, so instead of finishing my studies, I found myself standing in a long line of inductees waiting for my physical examination.

After the physical, I had to go into another room to be interviewed about my work experiences so the Army could figure out the best way to use me. I entered the room and was amazed to see that one of the officials interviewing the inductees was Jerry Nicholson, who had been

my roommate at Linfield College. We were so poor in those days that we had rented a small room and slept together in one bed. When Jerry spotted me, he motioned me to follow him. We went into his office, he shut the door, and we had a good reunion before we got down to business. "With your education," he told me, "I can get you a commission."

"Thanks a lot, Jerry," I said, "but I don't want to start out an officer. I am going to do like my grandfather Medicine Crow. My grandfather started his military career as a young man, worked his way up through the Crow warrior ranks, and became a great chief. I am going to follow in his footsteps."

It was the biggest mistake I ever made because the U.S. Army did not work on the principles of the Crow tribe. I entered the Army as a private and came out a private. I never got another chance to be an officer. In fact, at first I wasn't even a combat soldier. The Army assigned me to be a clerk, a paper pusher, and that is how I spent my first couple of years on active duty.

All that changed in the closing months of World War II. The Army needed foot soldiers for

the invasion of Germany, and I was one of those moved to the front lines. Here finally was my opportunity to be a warrior, to meet the enemy in combat. But, in truth, I knew little about being a warrior, only the stories I had heard growing up.

In the pre-reservation days, a young Crow man aspiring to be a warrior would go into the Wolf Teeth Mountains seeking *Baxbe*, or spiritual power. He believed that this power would make him a better warrior, make him more successful in performing war deeds, and help him eventually to become a chief with great wealth, high prestige, and a large following. The Crow called this spiritual experience "Going Without Water." Over three or four days of fasting, the young man hoped to receive a visit by animal spirits who were emissaries of the First Maker, or Great Spirit. Sometimes the vision seeker would cut off a finger, adding the pain of a blood sacrifice to his pangs of hunger and thirst.

The ordeal was voluntary, and not all young men believed they needed a personal vision experience to be a successful warrior. Some preferred to go directly to a veteran warrior or spiritual leader and get his blessing. Having been raised

Christian, I never attempted a traditional vision quest. I preferred to do my communicating with the First Maker in church. But I still believed in traditional sources of spiritual power.

During my tour of duty in Germany, I always carried with me a special feather that had belonged to a Shoshone Sun Dance chief from Fort Washakie. He had given it to my uncle Tom Yellowtail. It was a little, fluffy, snow white eagle feather. Before a battle, I would put the feather inside my helmet. In addition to carrying the feather, I recited certain prayers and painted myself with a red lightning streak and red ring. I did not put the paint on my face but on my arms under my shirt. My uncle taught me how to paint myself properly. If I did not have paint, I could use a red pencil. That worked as well as paint. When I was under fire, I felt much better because of my special spiritual "medicine."

To this day, I credit my medicine for saving my life during several close encounters with the Germans. One such encounter occurred when my company came under artillery and mortar fire while we were marching on the side of a narrow valley.

The Germans were directly across from us. We were sitting ducks, but I felt pretty well prepared. My knapsack was full of pemmican, a special treat of pounded meat that my mother had sent me. I had my rifle. I had painted the symbols on my arms, and I had put the medicine feather in my helmet.

Suddenly, everything went black. An artillery shell had exploded right in front of me. It killed or wounded about a half dozen of the soldiers nearest me. The blast knocked me right over the side of the cliff we were walking on. The hillside was very steep and covered with trees and rocks. I could hear guys moaning all around me. Miraculously, I was not hurt, just bruised a bit. But my helmet was gone. My medicine feather was gone. My knapsack with the pemmican was gone. My rifle was gone. I felt helpless. I was in shock.

It was now nighttime, and the hill was so steep, I couldn't walk. I had to crawl out of there. I began pulling myself up the hill by grabbing one tree and then another. First, I found my rifle. A little farther up the hill I found my knapsack. Near the last tree at the top of the hill, I found my helmet with the feather still tucked in the liner. When I put the helmet back on, I came to my senses. Everything was now all right, but I admit, I had panicked there for a while. I have always attributed that particular sequence of good luck to my special Indian medicine. Whenever I had a close call, I would think about that medicine.

After I returned from the war, I gave that feather to one of my cousins, Henry Old Coyote. He was a machine gunner on a B-25. That feather went with him to Africa, Germany, and Italy. I think after the Second World War that feather then went to Korea with a Crow soldier. It might have even gone to Vietnam. I don't know where it is now, but it certainly was powerful.

CHAPTER FIFTEEN

A Crow Warrior in Germany

NATURALLY, I THOUGHT ABOUT the famous warriors when I went to Germany. I had a legacy to live up to. My goal was to be a good soldier, to perform honorably in combat if the occasion should occur. I did not think in terms of counting coup. Those days were gone, I believed. But when I returned from Germany and the elders asked me and the other Crow veterans to tell our war stories, lo and behold, I had completed the four requirements to become a chief.

I accomplished my first coup when the allies—the United States, France, and Great Britain—started the big push into Germany from France. I was a private in Company K, 411th

Infantry, 103rd Division, known as the Cactus Division, a Texas outfit. I was the only Indian in my company.

It was January and the ground was covered with snow. The boundary that separated the two countries at this point was a little creek, about the size of Lodge Grass Creek, running through a canyon. It was a pretty deep canyon with steep walls. It was not rocky like our canyons in Montana, but it had real sharp hills. That was the border. The French Maginot line, with its big guns, was behind us. On the other side of this creek, facing us, were the big guns of the German Siegfried line.

Well, we went down the hill on the French side, crossed over into Germany, and started toward the Seigfried line. By now it was late afternoon. Before long we ran into foxholes just loaded with Germans. Then the fight started. After about an hour of fighting, it got dark, but we pushed forward. The Germans slowly withdrew up the side of their hill toward their big guns. As they retreated, we discovered a network of trenches higher than our heads and about three or four feet wide, going every which way. We took the main trench and followed it to the top of the hill, but it was tough going. The path was kind of steep, slushy, and muddy.

By the time I got to the top, the 30 or 40 of our boys who had gone ahead of me had made the ground even more sloppy and slippery. To make matters worse, the guy in front of me was a fat, clumsy kid. He was always slipping and falling. When we finally reached the crest of the hill, he couldn't make it over the top. He'd get there, almost to the top, then slide down. Finally, I managed to push him up and over. Just then, the Germans opened fire, and he came sliding back down again and landed on top of me. I think that is the only reason I didn't get killed that day. All the guys who had gotten on top were wiped out. The rest of us scattered. We went back down the hill into the side trenches.

The next day someone made the decision to blow up the pillboxes, large concrete bunkers with big guns, where the Germans were hiding. As luck would have it, I was standing next to the commanding officer when the order came over the telephone. The message said to send some men back up the hill on the French side to get the boxes of dynamite needed to blow up the pillboxes.

The CO said, “Well, Chief”—he always called me Chief—“I guess if anybody can get through, you can. Get six men and go up there.” Boy, it was a high hill, loaded with land mines, hidden bombs that would go off if you stepped on them.

Before I could ask for volunteers, my closest buddy stepped up and said, “Let’s go, Chief.” In all, six guys, my closest friends, went with me. I was glad only six came forward because that made seven of us, and seven is one of the numbers Indians consider lucky.

Before we left, the company commander ordered a smoke screen. “We can’t afford to let these guys go in plain sight,” he said. So guns from the American side began throwing smoke screen shells on the hill to give us cover. Pretty soon that whole hillside was covered with a mass of white smoke. Then we took off.

Meanwhile, the Germans realized something was happening, so they began lobbing mortar shells in our direction. We finally made it, but it took a long time crawling up that hill. It was steep and slippery with wet snow, but at least we did not set off any land mines or get hit by any mortar shells.

Anyhow, we finally got up there to the French side. The mess tent was still up, and so was the communication center. We were given some hot soup and coffee, but not much time to rest, maybe half an hour, before they told us to take off again. They gave us boxes of dynamite with fuses. Each box weighed 50 pounds. We tried putting them on our shoulders, but the edges cut into our shoulders. We couldn't walk down the hill carrying them in both hands. They were just too clumsy to handle.

I didn't know what to do at first. Then I just sat down, set my box on my knees, and started sliding down the hill. The other guys saw me and did the same thing. Here we were, sliding behind one another down that hill. It wasn't fast, but we made it.

Our boys had thrown some more smoke shells on the hillside to keep it foggy, but the Germans were lobbing mortar shells and hand grenades, too. If our boxes had gotten hit or if we had stepped on a mine, we would have been goners. It was a terrifying experience, but somehow we all came back without a scratch and with seven boxes of dynamite. The engineers then went ahead and blew up two or three of those big pillboxes.

When I later told this story to the elders, they told me it was the same as leading a war party in the olden days. I had been assigned to a command job. We had returned safely and victoriously. We hadn't come back with horses or scalps, but we had returned with materials essential to the welfare of our men. That was my first war deed.

My next war deed was counting coup on a German soldier. After attacking the Siegfried line, we were sent back to France for a couple of months of rest. Then, in March 1944, our unit went back into Germany. Soon after crossing the border we came to a little town.

Our assignment was to enter the town from the rear, while other units attacked straight on. Boy, it was cold. There was still snow on the ground. To approach the town we had to wade through a slough up to our chests. I tell you it was wet and it was cold, but it was the safest way to get into town because the Germans had planted land mines all over. Because the Germans never expected anyone to come from that direction, we entered without their noticing us. In the meantime, our boys who had gotten through the land mines had started hitting the other side of the town.

I had about five or six soldiers assigned to me. We were told to secure a particular back alley. Although there was a lot of gunfire in the main street, the back alley where I was going was kind of quiet. With my platoon right behind me, I began running down the alley. I was carrying an M1 rifle. Along one side of the alley was a stone wall about ten feet high. As I was running, I could see a gate, so I headed for it. I wanted to see what was happening on the main street.

A German soldier had the same idea, it turned out. He was running toward the gate, too, but from the other side of the wall. With all the shooting going on, I could not hear him, and he could not hear me either. We met at the gate.

My reactions were a bit quicker than his. I hit him under the chin with the butt of my rifle and knocked him down, sending his rifle flying. He tried to reach for his rifle, but I kicked it out of the way. I dropped my gun and jumped on top of him and put my hands around his throat.

Meanwhile, the rest of my guys had caught up. They wanted to shoot the German, but I still had my hands on his throat. He was scared. He began hollering, *"Hitler Kaput! Hitler Kaput! Hitler nicht gude!"* which meant, "Hitler dead! Hitler dead! Hitler no good!" He was crying. Tears were running down his face. I felt so sorry for him, I let him go.

Capturing that German counted for two war deeds. He was the first German we ran into that day, and by knocking him down and touching him, I had counted coup on him. I had also taken his weapon away from him, which was another coup.

Even though I wasn't thinking about counting coup, I had been looking for a chance to capture a horse. To me that was the best thing I could do to prove that I was worthy of my ancestors. The war was almost over before I finally got my chance at a German horse.

We were following a group of Hitler's SS officers who were on horseback, about 50 of them. They had abandoned their men, who were surrendering by the thousands. We followed these SS all night. They were riding their horses on an asphalt road, and we could hear the clop, clop of the hooves ahead of us. About midnight, the horsemen left the highway and went to a farm about three miles down a dirt road. We followed their trail in the moonlight and arrived at a villa with a barn and a little fenced pasture.

As our commanding officer sat down with the platoon leaders to discuss how best to handle the situation, all I could think about was those horses in the corral. The decision was made to attack the farmhouse at daybreak.

The next morning, when the CO finished telling the platoon leaders to take their men this way and that way, I said: "Sir, maybe I should get those horses out of the corral before you attack because some of those SS guys might be able to escape on them. It would only take me about five minutes." The CO looked at me funny for a second, but he probably had an idea of what I was up to. "Okay, Chief, you're on."

That was all I needed. I took one of my buddies, and we began sneaking down toward the corral and the barn. We had to be careful in case a German was in the barn on guard duty, watching. When we got there, nothing was moving. The horses were tired, just standing around. I crawled through the corral fence and came up to one of them. I told him, *"Whoa, whoa,"* in English.

He snorted a little bit, but he quickly settled down. I had this rope with me that I used to tie my blanket. I took that rope and tied his lower jaw with a double half hitch, just like the old-time Crow warriors used to do, and then I tried to get on. But it was a tall horse, and my boots were so muddy and caked up, I had a hard time mounting. Finally, I led the horse to the watering trough and stood on that to get on its back.

I had told my buddy that I was going to the other end of the paddock behind the horses, and as soon as I got there I would give a little whistle. When he heard the whistle, he was to open the gate and get out of the way. Well, I got back there and gave the whistle. Then I gave a Crow war cry, and those horses took off.

There were woods about half a mile away, so as soon as we cleared the gate, I headed in that direction. Just about then our boys opened fire on the farmhouse. By now it was coming daylight and I could get a good look at my horses. I had about 40 or 50 head. I was riding a sorrel with a blaze, a real nice horse. When we reached the woods and the horses started to mill around, I did something spontaneous. I sang a Crow praise song and rode around the horses. They all just looked at me.

The Germans had surrendered quickly, and the firing was over, so I left the horses in the woods except the one I was riding and headed back to the farmhouse.

After we had finished mopping things up and sending the prisoners to the rear, the company commander said, “Let’s go,” and we took off. There was a gravel railroad bed nearby, which made the walking a little better. As the guys took off down the railroad track, I was still on my horse.

It was better to ride than to walk. I felt good. I was a Crow warrior. My grandfathers would have been proud of me, I thought. But all too soon, the reality of the war came back. After letting me ride the horse for about a mile or so, the CO yelled over to me, “Chief, you better get off. You make too good a target.”

CHAPTER SIXTEEN

High Bird

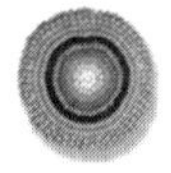

I WAS INDUCTED INTO THE ARMY March 4, 1943, and discharged January 10, 1946. I phoned my parents from Camp McCoy, Wisconsin, and said I would arrive in Lodge Grass by train Number 41 at 6 p.m. on January 15.

When Crow soldiers came home after serving in World War II, their relatives would stage a welcome at the train station and host a grand reception about a week or two later.

When I returned, my train stopped in Sheridan, Wyoming, for about 30 minutes, so I ran downtown to have a hamburger feed at Louie's. Louie could make a dime hamburger taste like a New York–cut sirloin. Boy, I sure missed those hamburgers while I was overseas.

It was a bad decision, however, because the train left without me.

In the meantime, a huge welcome crowd awaited me at the Lodge Grass train depot. My mother was ready with a stack of new Pendleton blankets to spread from the train to the singers some 60 feet away. As I stepped off the train, I was supposed to walk along the row of blankets and start dancing as I reached the singers. Well, this didn't take place. A woman on the train from Sheridan informed my mother that I was seen at Louie's with a big pile of burgers in front of me! Poor Mom, she sure must have been disappointed.

Anyhow, the reception was held that weekend. People were gathered in front of the dance hall when I arrived that Saturday afternoon. As I walked into the hall, people along the way shook my hands, relatives hugged me, and admiring girls kissed me. When I stepped into the hall, the drummers sang the war honor song of my grandfather Chief Medicine Crow. I danced around the floor with my relatives dancing behind me.

Several elders who were still familiar with intertribal military traditions requested my recital of my war deeds. This request took me unawares as I had never thought about my activities on the battlefield as "war deeds," except when I captured the horses. But I told the elders about my hand-to-hand encounter with the German soldier and how I took his gun away from him. Then I related the time I was in charge of the detail of soldiers that went after dynamite so the big guns along the Siegfried line could be blasted. And I told them about sneaking into the German camp and stealing the horses belonging to the SS officers. For those four coups, I was declared a full-fledged Crow war chief.

After the reciting of the war deeds, my folks and relatives started the giveaway, which is always done when someone in Crow society is honored. I know in white society when someone is honored, that person gets presents, but that is not the way it is done in Crow society. When someone succeeds, he or she gives presents to those who helped make that success possible, like parents, relatives, teachers, and friends. My mother gave away a stack of new Pendleton blankets, quilts, and other nice things. Then my stepdad, John White Man Runs Him, brought in a fine saddle horse with a new saddle and bridle and gave it away in my honor. The last event of the day was a big feast.

At that welcome home reception, I also got a new name. One of my Whistling Water clansmen, Ties His Knees, and some others got together and talked things over. They said, "Let's give Winter Man a new name. Let's name him after one of our illustrious Whistling Water men." So they gave me his name, High Bird. Of course, High Bird had died long before. They also gave me his honor song, and they gave me his right as an announcer, or town crier.

And my former name, Winter Man? Shortly after that, we had a dance at Lodge Grass. During the dance, another of my Whistling Water clan brothers, Elsworth Little Light, talked to the announcer for a while and then called me over. "Right now," he said, "I am going to buy your name for my son." His son was Robert Little Light. That's how it works. Someone can buy your name for himself or his son or some relative, and you can't refuse. So he took my name Winter Man and gave it to his son. He gave me several things—some money, a Pendleton blanket, and so forth—so I don't use that name anymore.

I still have the name Joe Medicine Crow, my legal name, so in the white world, I'm Joe. But among my Crow people, I am High Bird. We use our Indian names during dances, ceremonials, powwows, and other tribal events. And it is also at the tribal ceremonies that I use my honor song, which my Whistling Water clansmen gave me after World War II. When it is played, I dance and my relatives follow me. The words in my honor song, like the songs of the Crow chiefs before me, reflect the pride we Crow people cherish to this day for our warrior heroes.

High Bird, you are a great soldier!
High Bird, you fought the mighty Germans!
High Bird, you counted coup on them!
High Bird, you are a great soldier!

Bako Dagak!
Da Bachiak Icupe Uwatay!
Da Dichic Dakshay!
Bako Dagak!

Another
National Geographic book
you might enjoy!

Available in hardcover, paperback,
and reinforced library editions

Chapter One
A Lion Hunt

My sweet mother,
Don't call me a baby.
I stopped being a baby when I was initiated.

I'M GOING TO TELL you the lion story.

Where I live in northern Kenya, the lion is a symbol of bravery and pride. Lions have a special presence. If you kill a lion, you are respected by everyone. Other warriors even make up songs about how brave you are. So it is every warrior's dream to kill a lion at one point or another. Growing up, I'd had a lot of interaction with wild animals—elephants, rhinos, cape buffalo, hyenas. But at the time of this story—when I was about 14—I'd never come face-to-face with a lion, ever. I'd heard stories from all the young warriors who told me, "Wow, you know yesterday we chased this lion—" bragging about it. And I always said, "Big deal." What's the big deal about a lion? It's just an animal. If I can defend myself against elephants or rhinos, I thought, why not a lion?

I WAS JUST BACK from school for vacation. It was December, and there was enough rain. It was green and beautiful everywhere. The cows were giving plenty of milk. In order to get them away from ticks, the cattle had been taken down to the lowlands. There's good grass there, though it's drier than in the high country, with some rocks here and there. There are no ticks, so you don't have to worry about the health of the cattle, but the area is known for its fierce lions. They roam freely there, as if they own the land.

I spent two days in the village with my mom, then my brother Ngoliong came home to have his hair braided and asked me to go to the cattle camp along with an elder who was on his way there. I'd say the cattle camp was 18 to 24 miles away, depending on the route, through some rocky areas and a lot of shrubs. My spear was broken, so I left it at home. I carried a small stick and a small club. I wore my *nanga,* which is a red cloth, tied around my waist.

It took us all day to get there, but at sunset we

were walking through the gap in the acacia-branch fence that surrounded our camp. There were several cattle camps scattered over a five-mile radius. At night we could see fires in the distance, so we knew that we were not alone. As soon as we got there my brother Lmatarion told us that two lions had been terrorizing the camps. But lions are smart. Like thieves, they go somewhere, they look, they take, but they don't go back to the same place again.

Well, that was our unlucky day. That evening when the cows got back from grazing, we had a lot of milk to drink, so we were well fed. We sat together around the fire and sang songs—songs about our girlfriends, bravery songs. We swapped stories, and I told stories about school. The others were always curious to understand school. There were four families in the camp, but most of the older warriors were back at the village seeing their girlfriends and getting their hair braided. So there were only three experienced warriors who could fight a lion, plus the one elder who had come down with me. The rest of us were younger.

We went to bed around 11:30 or 12. We all slept out under the stars in the cattle camp—no bed, just a cowhide spread on bare soil. And at night it gets cold in those desert areas. For a cover I used the nanga that I had worn during the day. The piece of cloth barely covered my body, and I kept trying to make it longer and pull it close around me, but it wouldn't stretch. I curled myself underneath it trying to stay warm.

Everything was silent. The sky was clear. There was no sign of clouds. The fire was just out. The stars were like millions of diamonds in the sky. One by one everybody fell asleep. Although I was tired, I was the last to sleep. I was so excited about taking the cows out the following morning.

During the middle of the night, I woke to this huge sound—like rain, but not really like rain. I looked up. The starlight was gone, clouds were everywhere, and there was a drizzle falling. But that wasn't the sound. The sound was all of the cows starting to pee. All of them, in every direction. And that is the sign of a lion. A hyena doesn't make them do that. An elephant doesn't make them do that. A person doesn't. Only the lion. We knew right away that a lion was about to attack us.

If you want to read more about Lemasolai's adventures, ask your bookseller or librarian for *Facing the Lion*.